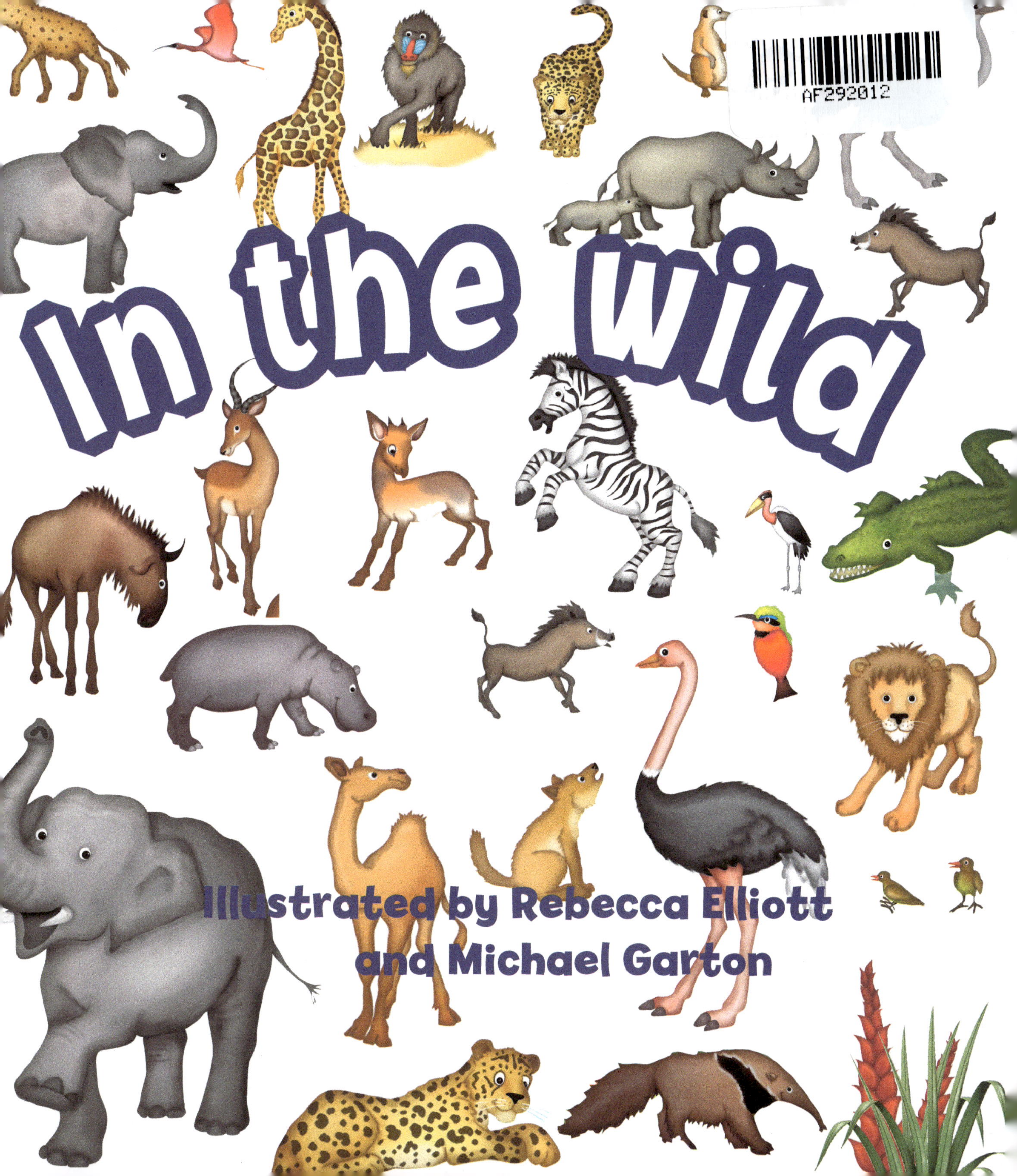

In the wild

Illustrated by Rebecca Elliott
and Michael Garton

2

All kinds of animals
live in the wild.
Let's find out who
they are.

Many live on the wide open
grasslands where they graze
in herds. Some hide in
the trees or burrow in the
ground.

Let's meet them all.

Herds of deer

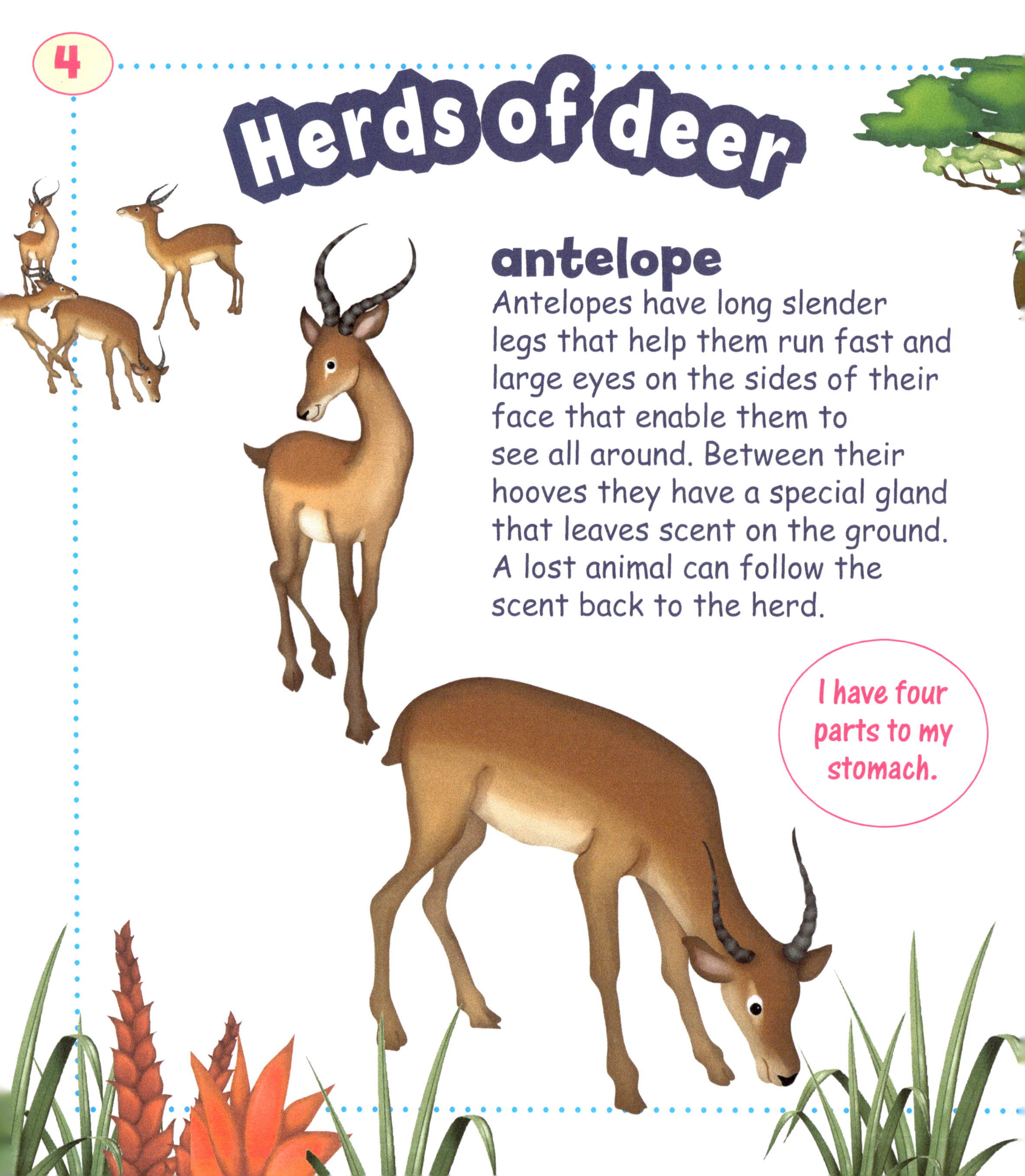

antelope

Antelopes have long slender legs that help them run fast and large eyes on the sides of their face that enable them to see all around. Between their hooves they have a special gland that leaves scent on the ground. A lost animal can follow the scent back to the herd.

dik-dik

A dik-dik is a very small type of deer. Dik-diks are only about 30 to 40 centimetres high, making it easy for them to hide from enemies in tall grass.

In the desert

camel

Camels live in dry sandy places such as deserts. Their feet have pads that stop them from sinking into the sand. Camels store food as fat in the humps on their backs.

dromedary

A dromedary is a kind of camel but it has one hump on its back and not two.

On the grassy plain

wildebeest

A wildebeest is a kind of large antelope. It lives in herds on the grassland of Africa. It has a long head and a hairy mane. A herd can migrate hundreds of kilometres to find food.

Huge elephants

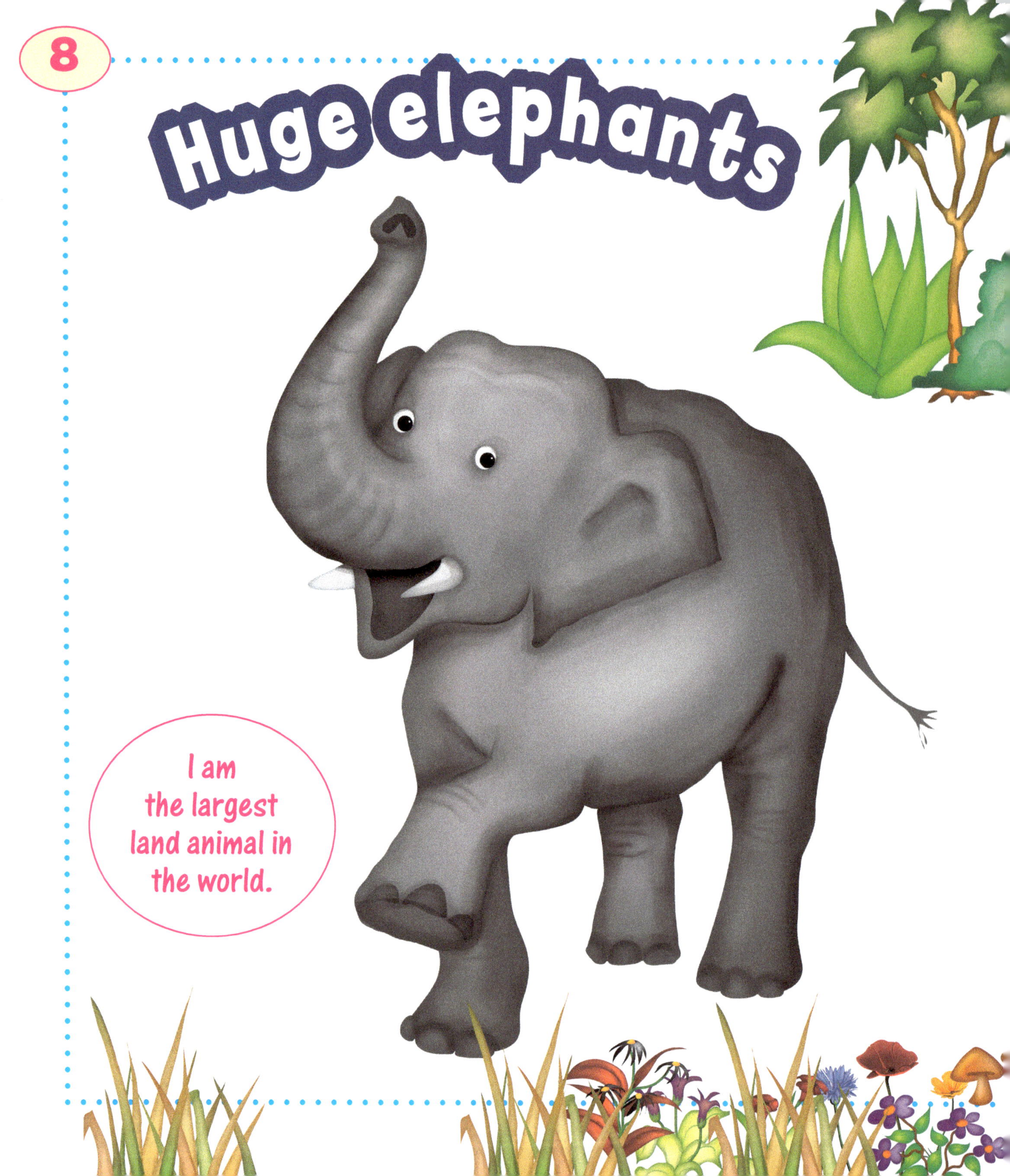

elephant

Elephants live in herds of 15 to 30 animals. The females help to care for each others' babies. An elephant drinks up to 200 litres of water a day.

Hunting family

dingo

The dingo may be an ancestor of the grey wolf. It has a short sandy-coloured or gingery red coat. It feeds on rabbits, rodents and even kangaroos. Dingos live and hunt in packs.

Burrowing family

meerkat

Meerkats have long claws on their front feet to dig burrows and scratch for food such as insects and small animals. They live in groups of up to 30 animals. They stand on their hind legs to act as look-out.

Big cat

lion

Lions live in a group of four to six females and their cubs called a pride. A pride has its own territory. The lions work together to catch prey such as zebra and wildebeest. You can tell a male lion by its shaggy mane.

Fierce hunters

leopard

Leopards have light brown coats with dark spots. This helps them hide while they sneak up on their prey. When they have finished eating they haul their leftover meat into a tree and leave it there to eat later.

cheetah

The cheetah is a wild cat. Its slender body and long legs help it run at 110 kilometres an hour. It hunts gazelles, wildebeest and hares.

Tall legs

ostrich

The ostrich is the largest bird in the world. It is too big to fly but it is a fast runner on its two legs and can move at 65 kilometres an hour.

rhea

Rheas are like ostriches but they are grey-brown all over. They live on the grasslands of South America.

flamingo

The beautiful flamingo lives in the lakes and marshes of Africa. Thousands of flamingos live together in flocks. When they eat, they filter shellfish and tiny animals through their long beaks.

stork

Storks wade in shallow, fresh water on their long legs. They use their sharp beaks to quickly grab fish or frogs that come close. Storks build their nests in tall trees or on the ground.

crane

Cranes have long legs and long necks. They keep their necks stretched out when they fly.

Long snouts

anteater

The anteater feeds on small insects. Many, such as ants, have a sting, so the anteater must suck them from the anthill very quickly on its long tongue. It can flick its tongue 150 times a minute.

warthog

The warthog is a kind of pig. It lives in the forests of Africa. It has several wart-like knobs of skin on its face. The warthog grows two pairs of curved tusks. It has a long mane of hair.

tapir

A tapir is related to a horse and a rhinoceros. It has a thick body, short legs and a short, flexible trunk. It lives in the tropical rainforests.

Tough trouble

hippopotamus

On land, a hippopotamus looks clumsy but it can run fast. It spends most of its time under the water, with just its eyes, ears and nostrils above the surface. It swims or runs along the bottom of the river or lake.

At night I graze on grass.

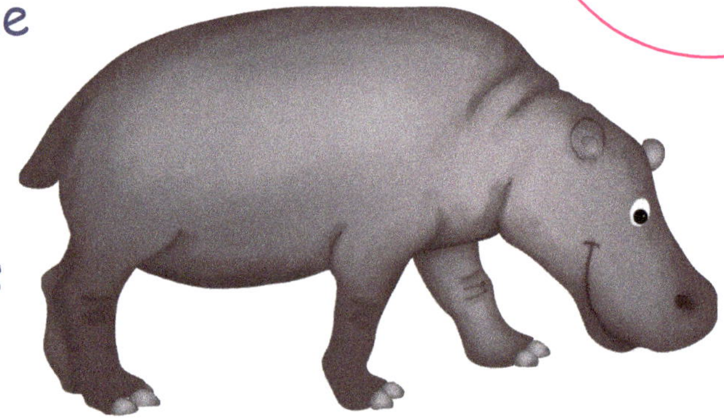

Beware my sharp teeth!

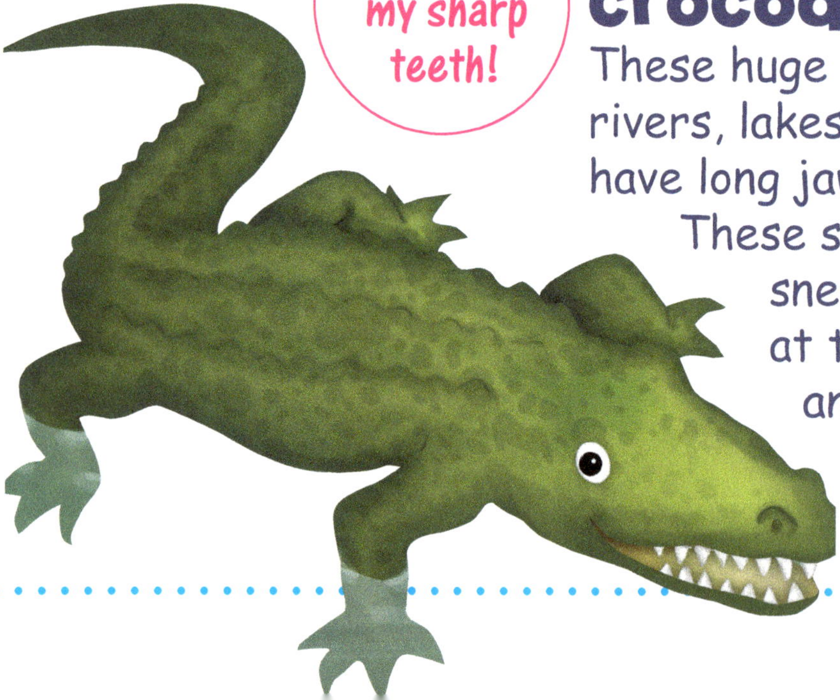

crocodile

These huge reptiles live in rivers, lakes and lagoons. They have long jaws and sharp teeth. These stealthy hunters sneak up on their prey at the water's edge and attack.

rhinoceros

The rhinoceros is a large animal with thick skin, short, strong legs and hoofed feet. On the front of its head are one or two horns made of keratin, a tough protein found in nails and hair.

Stripes in the grass

zebra

This striped mammal is related to the horse and lives in eastern and southern Africa. A zebra's coat has bold black and white stripes and it has a stiff mane along its neck. It lives in herds and grazes on grass.

Reaching high

giraffe

The long-necked giraffe is the tallest animal in the world. It can grow five and a half metres high. Giraffes eat leaves, twigs and fruits which they pluck from tall trees.

Who can you see?

23
Who can
you see?
Who can
you see?

The animals I met

Aa	anteater	**Hh**	hippopotamus
	antelope	**Ll**	leopard
Cc	camel		lion
	cheetah	**Mm**	meerkat
	crane	**Oo**	ostrich
	crocodile	**Rr**	rhea
Dd	dik-dik		rhinoceros
	dingo	**Ss**	stork
	dromedary	**Tt**	tapir
Ee	elephant	**Ww**	warthog
Ff	flamingo		wildebeest
Gg	giraffe	**Zz**	zebra